Weather Wits & Science Snickers

by Steve LaNore

Introduction

Perhaps you think science is boring and complicated with people using lots of big words on purpose, but that's just what they show on TV. What it's really about is discovery. If you ever wonder how or why something happens, then you've already cracked open the door to a world of endless potential.

Science is everywhere…from proper placement of a home weather station to scanning a thunderstorm with radar to designing the sensors for NASA's Mars Curiosity Rover.

If the words and pictures in this book help you appreciate what a fascinating world we live in and what a big part science plays, then my mission is accomplished. And if you get a few laughs along the way, so much the better!

Enjoy,

Steve LaNore

Pottsboro, Texas

October 2012

Table of Contents

Things in the Sky..1

   Alaskan Electric Bills...3

   Halo Around the Moon..6

   Bogus Raindrops...8

   Can't Pay Attention..10

Things on the Ground...13

   A Messy Weather Map..14

   No Money...16

   Ants and Radar..18

   Dinosaur Bones..21

   Scientists Play Guitar...23

   Pizza, Please...25

Dust and Danger..29

   Tornado Adventures..30

   Tornado Watch..33

   "Hot" Deal on a Used Car...35

   Blackmail in the Desert..37

   A Bite without Teeth...39

Sun and Space...41

   Jupiter Goes to the Doctor..42

   Let's Fly to the Sun...44

   The Dumb Astronaut...46

   Spaceship and Rocket..48

   Three-Part Joke...50

Discovery Websites...52

Resources..53

Words of Thanks..56

About the Author...57

Things in the Sky

Alaskan Electric Bills

Q: Why don't Alaskans have electric bills?

A: Because they use the Northern Lights.

What are the Northern Lights?

Super-charged particles stream out from the sun all of the time, and this is called the solar wind. The solar wind is strongest when there are lots of sunspots on the sun's surface. When the charged particles get close to the Earth, our magnetic field steers them toward the north and south poles. They then hit the Earth's upper atmosphere, and molecules of oxygen and nitrogen gas give off light as the energy strikes them.

Yellow-green is the most common color of aurora and it's produced by oxygen molecules that are located about 60 miles above the Earth. All-red auroras are produced by oxygen at greater heights, up to about 200 miles. Nitrogen molecules give off blue or purplish-red auroras at all altitudes.

Alaska, Canada, and northern Europe offer the most amazing Northern Light displays, but they have been sighted as far south as Texas and Florida during stronger solar events.

Here are three excellent examples of the northern lights in action:

Des Moines, IA / Stan Richard

Tromso, Norway / Bjorn Jorgensen

Nitrogen molecules lighting up the arctic sky.

Halo around the Moon

Q: How can you tell when the moon has been on good behavior?

A: It's got a halo around it.

What makes a halo?

High clouds more than 15,000 feet above sea level are made up of tiny ice crystals. They are not shaped like ice cubes in your freezer, but come in "weird" shapes like stretched-out hexagons. Light is bent (refracted) passing through the crystals, and when enough of the crystals are present in a cloud, a halo is born.

Halos can be seen around the moon or the sun. The ones around the moon are easier to see and, of course, you should NEVER look directly at the sun! Moon halos are made of sunlight since the moon has no light source of its own.

A typical moon halo / National Weather Service image

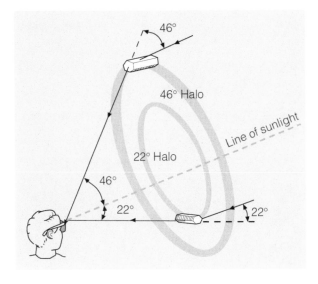

The moonlight (which comes from the sun as shown here) is bent passing through 6-sided ice crystals found in cirrus clouds to create the illusion of a halo. A larger 46-degree halo may also occur, but they are less common.

Bogus Raindrops

Q: How can you tell when a raindrop is rude?

A: It drops in uninvited.

Raindrops don't look like teardrops. Why?

Most cartoons and TV weathercasts show raindrops shaped like tears. Did you know they don't really look like that? Small raindrops start out pretty much round in shape. The drop falls through the air and its shape is "bent" by air friction as it gets bigger, making it look more like a hamburger bun than a teardrop!

Friction breaks up the drop when it gets to about two-tenths of an inch across and the whole cycle starts over. It may sound like the rain is falling at 60 mph when it's really pouring, but unless you're in a storm with a strong downdraft, a typical downpour contains raindrops falling at about 15 mph.

Hamburger-bun shaped raindrops would probably look weird on a weather map, so I suppose that we'll keep drawing them the wrong way since "real" raindrops don't look as cool. Watch out for the science police!

Can't Pay Attention

Q: Why do weather students have a hard time paying attention in class?

A: They have their heads in the clouds.

How do clouds form?

The next time you see the sky filled with cottony white clouds, picture a big bubble of rising air inside each one. It will help you understand what's going on inside of it. Each cloud is made by a pocket of rising air that cools. As it cools, the invisible moisture inside of it begins to appear as it condenses. It's the same process that makes a cold glass of ice tea "sweat" on a hot day.

The most common source of rising air is daytime heating, but cold fronts, wind blowing over mountains, cold air on top of warmer air, or frontal boundaries all work to make air rise too. When air rises with enough moisture present, clouds and sometimes rain and snow will form.

Cumulus clouds are a typical scene in the spring or summer sky. If conditions are right, a cumulus turns into a cumulonimbus (thunderstorm) cloud.

Cumulus clouds and fog at Whistler, Canada / site of the 2010 Winter Olympics

Cumulus over the mountainous western United States / Carl Wozniak

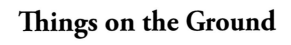
Things on the Ground

A Messy Weather Map

Q: How do you know when a weather map needs cleaning?

A: A cold front sweeps through.

Why are cold fronts important to weather?

A front is a dividing line that separates two kinds of air. It's not a solid surface like a wall in your house, but a zone of temperature, wind, and humidity change. A very strong front may bring sharp temperature drops, gusty wind, and rain or snow; a weak front will be less noticeable to you, but it can still be found by meteorologists on a map.

Knowing when a front will pass helps you plan outdoor activities and what to wear. The weather around fronts affects lots of jobs like pilots, truck drivers, and construction workers, so it's important for them to know when one is coming.

A "cold" front means the colder air is replacing the warmer air. A cold front is drawn as a blue line with teeth on a map, and it may be thousands of miles long. The front gently slopes into the sky on top of the cool air. Warmer air glides up this slope and clouds and rain form if conditions are right. If you were able to walk on the cold front as it went upward, it would take you about 100 miles of walking to reach a point along the front one mile above the Earth's surface. I'm tired just thinking about that!

A typical cold front, isobars and high pressure on a surface map.

No Money

Q: What type of bank is very large but never contains any money?

A: A fog bank.

How does fog form?

Have you ever seen a ring of water form on a table after a cold glass is placed on it? The glass is not leaking, so where is the water coming from? It's coming from the air. There is a gas called water vapor in the air all of the time, even in the driest deserts. When there's a lot of water vapor in the air, we say it's humid. When humid air touches something cold, the water vapor gas condenses into water drops, which we see on the glass. This same process makes the grass wet with dew (or frost, if it's cold enough) on some mornings.

Fog is a cloud on the ground. Clouds form due to condensation of water vapor into billions of tiny water droplets. Fog droplets are extremely small at about one one-hundredth of a millimeter. That's way smaller than the thickness of a human hair: Very tiny stuff.

Ground fog and frost on an Oklahoma winter morning.

Ants and Radar

Q: What do weather radar and ants have in common?

A: They both have antennas!

How does radar find rain?

Ants use two antennae attached to their heads to feel around for food, navigate, and to detect friends and enemies. Weather radar has one very large antenna which transmits and receives energy, and it works off of the same energy source which cooks food in a microwave oven.

The microwave in your home is about 1,000 watts; the radar uses around 750,000 watts!

Weather radar is focused in a very narrow beam to concentrate the energy in one direction. The antenna gradually scans up and down through the sky as it rotates to give a complete picture of storms, not just the bottom part.

When the radar beam hits a thunderstorm, millions of raindrops bounce some of the energy to the radar antenna. The returned energy is a low amount, but the sensitive equipment can pick this up. The technology used in radar allows storm warnings for tornadoes, hail and wind to be much more accurate than 40 years ago, and that saves lives.

This is a typical weather radar dish; it's portable, but they all have a similar appearance. NASA photo.

The radar antenna is usually covered by a fiberglass dome to prevent hail, wind, ice and snow effects. / CCSU

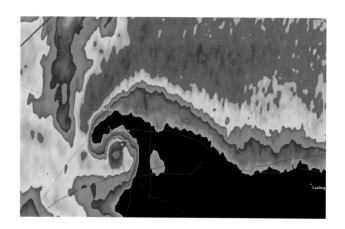 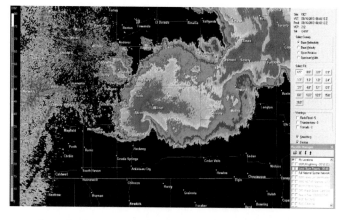

The image on the left shows the monster Tuscaloosa tornado of 2011; the one on the right shows a 2010 Kansas tornado. The red colors show very heavy rain, the green shows lighter rain, and the yellow is in between. Both storms shows the classic "hook" indicating strong rotation.

Dinosaur Bones

Q: Why did the guy put dinosaur bones in his gas tank?

A: He saw a TV report that said cars run on fossil fuels.

Does oil really come from fossils?

Oil, coal and natural gas are called "fossil fuels" because they are made from ancient plant and animal remains. The remains were buried and slowly transformed by pressure and heat into oil, coal or natural gas over millions of years.

Some oil-rich areas of the world like Saudi Arabia and Texas were once shallow seas where huge numbers of tiny sea creatures lived. They sank to the ocean floor after they died and formed thick layers of material that were gradually compressed and changed into fossil fuels. Ancient forests and swamps were sometimes turned into coal, oil or gas too. Dead trees and other plants fell into the water and formed many layers of material over a long time. A volcanic eruption, flood or landslide covered the layers and insulated them from oxygen in the air above. Pressure, heat, and time work in the same way to make fossil fuels from either plants or animals.

Most dinosaurs didn't have a chance to become oil because they died and decayed on the Earth's surface instead of getting buried, crushed, and heated. Sinclair Oil Company uses the dinosaur on its logo because oil is millions of years old and it makes for interesting advertising, but if there's any dinosaur in your tank it's a tiny amount.

Scientists Play Guitar

Q: Why do geologists make great guitarists?

A: They know how to rock.

What do geologists do?

Geology is the study of rocks inside the Earth and on its surface. Geologists have to learn how more than 1,000 minerals are put together and be able to identify them. They also have to learn how many different kinds of rock form layers in the Earth's crust. Each one is made in a different way.

Geologists find oil and precious metals like gold, and they study earthquakes and volcanoes. The prediction of earthquakes and volcanoes is getting better and it's because of the work geologists and other scientists are doing all of the time. Many lives have already been saved by warning people of these destructive and dangerous events.

Rocks are formed under high temperatures and pressures. Rocks made from many layers of material stacked one on another are called sedimentary rocks. These can be made of soil, plant and animal remains, or various minerals. Coal is a sedimentary rock, and so is rock salt. Igneous rocks start as liquid magma inside a volcano or lava that erupts from one. They may slowly cool and harden underground, or form quickly after an eruption. The rock shown below is an igneous rock.

Enchanted Rock west of Austin, TX is a huge dome of pink granite 425 feet high. It formed underground and was slowly exposed over millions of years by wind and water erosion. Photo by Jujutacular

Pizza, Please

Q: What type of pizza did the Earth order?

A: One with a thick crust.

What is the Earth's crust like?

All human beings live on the crust of the Earth. You want extra cheese with that?

The Earth's crust is made of huge "plates" of rock that fit together like giant puzzle pieces. The meeting points of the plates are called faults. Earthquakes happen when the intense pressures along the fault are suddenly released, like a giant spring. Undersea quakes can move trillions of gallons of seawater and sometimes create a tsunami like the one that hit Japan in 2011. The crust "stretches" apart at some places on Earth and these weak spots are also home to earthquakes.

There's a huge pool of semi-liquid rock below the crust called the mantle. It's more than a thousand miles from top to bottom and encircles our entire world. It runs about 2,000 degrees Fahrenheit—that's about five times hotter than your oven gets when you cook a Thanksgiving turkey.

Material from the mantle makes it to the surface through openings in the crust called volcanoes. Most of Earths' volcanoes can be found in an area where they also get earthquakes, because faults help make "soft" spots in the crust. When the liquid rock from the mantle pushes into the chamber below a volcano we call it magma. Magma can also be made by intense friction along a fault zone. We call magma "lava" after it erupts from the volcano. That's some hot pizza sauce!

The San Andreas Fault in California is clearly seen from the air. / Ian Kluft

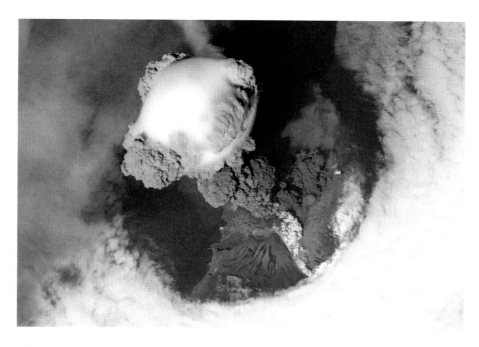

Sarychev volcano on the Russian coast erupting in 2009, as viewed from the International Space Station. / NASA

Dust and Danger

Tornado Adventures

Q: Did you hear of the man who wrote tornado adventures?

A: Yeah, the plots were really twisted.

What is a tornado?

Tornadoes form as a result of wind shear, which is when wind blows at different speeds, directions, or both as you go upward. These changing wind currents help the air to spin. If the air begins to rise quickly like in a thunderstorm, wind shear may get the whole storm spinning and produce a tornado.

Tornadoes can be very small, say 40 feet across, up to the world record of two and a half miles across. The average tornado is about 200 yards across and may have winds of 110 mph or so. Their speed across the ground (forward speed) ranges from 0–70 mph, but 20–30 mph is average. You cannot outrun them on foot most of the time, and that's a terrible idea anyway.

The most intense tornadoes have winds of 200–300 mph. These monsters are not that common, but they cause most tornado deaths. A mega-outbreak of huge tornadoes killed over 300 people during April 25–28, 2011 across several states from Arkansas to Alabama. It was the deadliest outbreak of tornadoes since the 1930s.

Doug Drace / Texoma Storm Chasers photo

Doug Drace / Texoma Storm Chasers photos

These images show an intense tornado over southwestern Oklahoma in November 2011. Winds in this funnel reached 175 mph and produced damage, but luckily no one was hurt. There's a second funnel appearing on the right in the image above. It's very rare to see twisters this large in November. Most big tornadoes happen during spring from March to June.

Tornado Watch

Q: Did you hear about the guy who walked up to the jewelry counter and asked for a tornado watch?

A: Yeah, it was an embarrassing "time" for him.

Tornado Watches and Warnings: What's all the fuss about?

A Tornado Watch means the National Weather Service (NWS) suspects dangerous weather and possibly tornadoes may form in your area within a few hours. A Tornado Warning means tornadic weather has already formed. "Tornadic" just means rotating. It comes from the Spanish word "tornar", which means "to turn."

Tornado Warnings are issued when Doppler radar picks up rotating storms or when a spotter reports one. There are sometimes false alarms with radar-only (no eyewitness) Tornado Warnings because a storm may show strong rotation and never put a tornado on the ground. Violent storms that don't produce a tornado often produce high wind and large hail, so they are still bad news. By the way, the word for tornado in Japanese is "tatsu maki".

Tornado with lightning bolt near Bouse Junction, OK / 14 April 2012

"Hot" Deal on a Used Car

Q: What do deserts and pushy people have in common?

A: They are both full of hot air.

Why are there deserts?

Most deserts have mountains around them that block air flow from the sea. The lack of moisture helps to make some deserts very hot because dry air heats up more than "wet" air.

The hottest *air* temperature ever measured on Earth was in Libya on September 13, 1922. It reached 136 degrees that day in the African desert. The rocks of the Lut Desert in Iran are even hotter: satellites measured a *ground* temperature of 160 degrees there. The image below was captured from the LANDSAT-7 satellite and it shows the especially hostile Lut Desert. The large brownish-colored area of sand and rocks on the left side of the image is where the extreme temperatures take place.

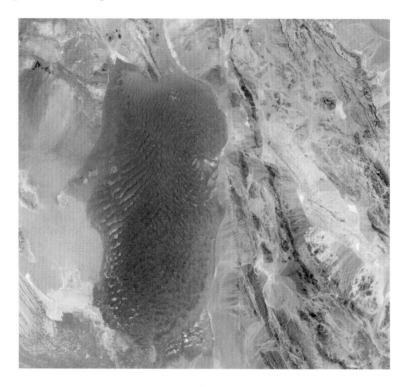

NASA images

There are polar deserts too. At the South Pole, less than two inches of snow falls per year, which easily qualifies it as a desert. Even two inches of snow a year can compress into enormous ice sheets over time. The Antarctic Ice Cap averages about 7,000 feet in thickness and is up to 11,000 feet thick in spots. The ice at the bottom is up to half a million years old! The image below is of Antarctica's vast Recovery Glacier.

Blackmail in the Desert

Q: How did the desert get a million dollars by blackmailing the dust devil?

A: It had all the dirt on him.

Is a dust devil just a dirty tornado?

No, but they do resemble one. Dust devils need warmer air at ground level for their updraft while a tornado can form day or night if the winds are right. Dust devils do not form at night because the sun provides the heat needed to get them going, and a dust devil is not attached to a cloud like a tornado.

A big one might be as wide as the length of a football field, but that's rare; 10 to 50 feet across is more typical. They are usually less than 1,000 feet high. A few very intense dust devils have damaged buildings with 75 mph winds, but winds in most of them are less than 40 mph. They won't cause major problems, but they'll give you a sand sandwich for sure! A dust devil will quickly fizzle once it loses its source of hot air. The biggest ones form in desert areas but they can show up almost anywhere over land.

Near Eloy, Arizona / NASA photo

A Bite without Teeth

Riddle: It has no teeth, but can be deadly when it sinks deep into your flesh. What is it?

A: Frostbite.

What is frostbite, and how can I keep from getting it?

Exposed skin can freeze in just a few minutes if it's cold enough outside. If it's 32 degrees or less, a strong wind speeds up the freezing process because the heat is carried away from the skin faster. The cooling effect of the wind is called the wind chill factor.

You can keep from getting frostbite by wearing proper clothing like gloves, a thick coat, and layers of clothes under the coat. Proper shoes are also very important. Don't forget a hat: 20% of your body heat escapes through your head. Ears, toes, and fingers are usually the first things to freeze. Stay indoors if the wind chill is very low.

Look at the chart below; choose the air temperature from the top row and then match it up with the wind speed on the left side. Move across to the intersection of the two points and that's the wind chill. Exposed flesh can freeze in just a few minutes when the wind chill is zero or less, and in less than one minute when the wind chill is minus 20 degrees or lower. Bundle up!

Flesh cannot freeze when it's above 32 degrees, but you can lose enough heat to get hypothermia. Hypothermia happens when your body's inside temperature falls below 95 degrees, and can be fatal. Your normal body temperature is around 98.6 degrees.

		Air Temperature (Degrees F)													
	calm	40	35	30	25	20	15	10	5	0	-5	-10	-15	-20	-25
		Apparent Temperature													
Wind Speed (MPH)	5	36	31	25	19	13	7	1	-5	-11	-16	-22	-28	-34	-40
	10	34	27	21	15	9	3	-4	-10	-16	-22	-28	-35	-41	-47
	15	32	25	19	13	6	0	-7	-13	-19	-26	-32	-39	-45	-51
	20	30	24	17	11	4	-2	-9	-15	-22	-29	-35	-42	-48	-55
	25	29	23	16	9	3	-4	-11	-17	-24	-31	-37	-44	-51	-58
	30	28	22	15	8	1	-5	-12	-19	-26	-33	-39	-46	-53	-60
	35	28	21	14	7	0	-7	-14	-21	-27	-34	-41	-48	-55	-62
	40	27	20	13	6	-1	-8	-15	-22	-29	-36	-43	-50	-57	-64
	45	26	19	12	5	-2	-9	-16	-23	-30	-37	-44	-51	-58	-65

National Weather Service data

Sun and Space

Jupiter Goes to the Doctor

Q: Why did the planet Jupiter go to the doctor?

A: It had a Great Red Spot to get rid of.

What is the "Great Red Spot"?

When Giovanni Cassini looked through his telescope in the year 1665, he discovered a huge whirlpool on Jupiter. The storm, called the "Great Red Spot," is still there!

No storm on Earth lasts more than a month or so, but the weather on Jupiter is vastly different from ours. The air currents around Jupiter are very fast but don't change much. The Great Red Spot is like a huge gear trapped between two conveyor belts of atmosphere going in opposite directions. It's been there at least 350 years.

Jupiter is extremely cold and has a poisonous atmosphere of hydrogen, helium, ammonia, and methane. It's not a very inviting place for a vacation—the average high temperature is 200 degrees below zero. Scientists also believe there is no solid surface on the planet, just huge seas of liquid hydrogen. Yeech!

The Great Red Spot is on the right side below the equator. Jupiter's moon Europa is casting a shadow onto the lower left portion of the planet / NASA image

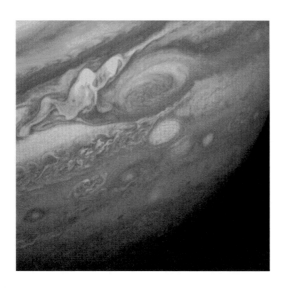

Close-up of the Great Red Spot / NASA

Let's Fly to the Sun

Story: Three scientists worked for years to design a manned solar probe. With much excitement they sent the project to NASA for consideration. After waiting several months, they had heard nothing, so they called. The NASA boss asked them, "Don't you know the intense temperature of the sun would destroy the spacecraft and doom the crew?" "Well," said the scientists, "No problem, because we're going to send them at night!"

What goes on inside the sun?

The sun is basically a huge nuclear explosion that never stops. Scientists estimate temperatures inside the sun are several million degrees. The sun's surface "cools" to 8,000–10,000 degrees, but temperatures above the sun's surface rise again to over a million degrees!

Huge magnetic fields on the sun's surface called sunspots follow a repeating pattern from low to high activity every 11 years or so. The sunspots occasionally "snap" and release solar flares. Solar flares and the Northern Lights are connected - when sunspots are numerous there are more auroras and there's less aurora activity when sunspots are fewer. The two images of solar flares shown below are from NASA's SOHO Observatory.

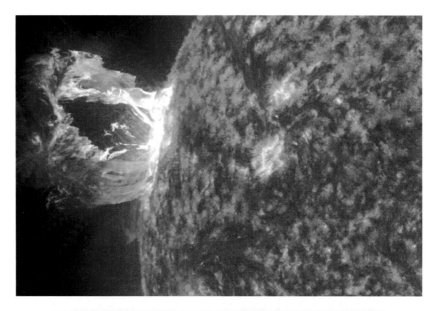

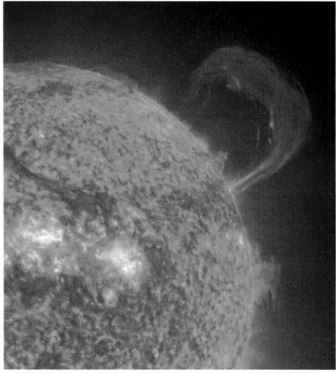

The Dumb Astronaut

Q: How did the really dumb astronaut try to collect lunar samples?

A: With a vacuum cleaner!

Why won't vacuum cleaners work in space?

Did you know that air is pushing on you all of the time? It's the weight of our atmosphere above being pulled earthward by gravity. If you climb a mountain, the air gets thinner and the pressure drops. There's a law that airlines must have oxygen for all passengers above 15,000 feet because the air is too thin to breathe. The air thins even more as you head into space until there is none at all. Scientists have found small particles of dust and gas in the void of outer space, but there's no air pressure. We call this a vacuum.

Your "vacuum cleaner" really doesn't make a vacuum. The fan creates an area of low pressure behind it, and the air in the room rushes into the hose to balance the pressure difference. So, it's actually the air in the room you're cleaning that picks up the dirt.

A vacuum cleaner can't do anything without air, so it is useless on the moon. A vacuum cleaner also doesn't work very well if you press it against a pillow because the air flow is mostly blocked. Try it yourself, but don't leave it there very long or you might damage the machine. Plus, it gets real noisy!

There's no air on the moon, so good luck with a vacuum cleaner! / NASA image

Spaceship and Rocket

Q: What did the rocket say to the spaceship after reaching orbit?

A: Man, I'm exhausted!

How do rockets get into space?

When a rocket takes off, it looks like the exhaust rushing out of the bottom is pushing it into the sky, but this is not what's happening. Isaac Newton discovered that for every action there is an equal and opposite reaction, so when the gases and flames gush out of the bottom of the rocket, an equal forward push is created. The force that moves a rocket is called thrust. A big rocket like the Saturn V used for the Apollo moon missions (shown below) generates seven million pounds of thrust!

Rockets used on long flights do not burn their engine all of the time. Since there is no friction in space and less gravity further away from Earth, a rocket can coast long after the engine is turned off. The Apollo lunar missions coasted for about three days once they escaped Earth's gravity before they fired a retro-rocket to slow the spacecraft and begin orbiting the moon. The Mars missions are in coast mode for many months before they reach the red planet.

Apollo 15 headed to the moon atop a Saturn V rocket, July 26, 1971 / NASA

Three-Part Joke

Q: What sucks? A vacuum cleaner.

Q: Okay, what really sucks? A tornado.

Q: Okay, what really, *really* sucks? A black hole!

How can a black hole use suction in the vacuum of space?

There are two kinds of suction: the first is when a liquid like water or a gas like air moves from higher to lower pressure. Examples include a swimming pool pump and a tornado. A tornado uses high wind velocity and low pressure to pull things into it—like a huge vacuum cleaner. There's no bag in a tornado, though.

The second kind of suction is caused by gravity and is used by planets, stars, and black holes. The larger or denser an object is, the stronger it pulls on surrounding objects with its gravitational force. A black hole is so dense that it actually pulls light into it, along with everything else that gets too close. You would not survive such a trip.

You might say the joke's on us when it comes to black holes.

An incredibly powerful black hole that is 70 million times more massive than our sun lies in the center of spiral galaxy M81 / NASA image

Discovery Websites

Check out more weather and science stuff with these info-packed weather and science links.

eo.ucar.edu/webweather/activities.html

Web weather for kids: experiments, info and generally a pretty cool place

weatherquestions.com

Huge alphabetical list of questions; graphics, easy to understand

weather.rap.ucar.edu

Great website for current maps, satellite and radar imagery, and model output in map form

spc.noaa.gov

Storm Prediction Center (SPC): Severe weather forecasts, storm reports, and historic data

nhc.noaa.gov

National Hurricane Center

apod.nasa.gov/apod

NASA astronomy picture of the day...index and archive to hundreds of fantastic images

usgs.gov

United States Geological Survey: Earthquake and volcano information

volcanolive.com

Volcano news and history

Topic Resources

Northern lights:

Bjorn Jorgensen's Norway auroras: arcticphoto.no

More northern lights images: bit.ly/K6bThF

Halos:

coolcosmos.ipac.caltech.edu/cosmic_kids/AskKids/moonring.shtml

In depth: hyperphysics.phy-astr.gsu.edu/hbase/atmos/halo22.html

Raindrops:

ga.water.usgs.gov/edu/raindropshape.html

Clouds:

eo.ucar.edu/webweather/cloud3.html

www.crh.noaa.gov/lmk/?n=cloud_classification

Cold Fronts:

okfirst.mesonet.org/train/meteorology/Fronts.html

Fog:

crh.noaa.gov/jkl/?n=fog_types

Radar:

weatherquestions.com/How_does_weather_radar_work.htm

bit.ly/Q1NdWs

srh.noaa.gov/lch/?n=ikemain (click under "radar imagery" section)

Fossil fuels:

science.howstuffworks.com/environmental/energy/oil-drilling.htm

energyquest.ca.gov/story/chapter08.html

Rocks:

fi.edu/fellows/fellow1/oct98/create/index.html

Earthquakes and volcanoes:

earthquake.usgs.gov/learn/kids/eqscience.php

umdrive.memphis.edu/g-sig/www/volcanoes.htm

Tornadoes:

noaanews.noaa.gov/2011_tornado_information.html

spc.noaa.gov/climo/online/monthly/newm.html

nssl.noaa.gov/edu/safety/tornadoguide.html

nssl.noaa.gov/primer/tornado/images/tor_formation_lg.jpg

ncdc.noaa.gov/oa/climate/severeweather/tornadoes.html

Deserts and Dust Devils:

weatherquestions.com/What_are_dust_devils.htm

indiana.edu/~geol116/Week11rainshad.jpg

mapsofworld.com/world-desert-map.htm

Frostbite and Hypothermia:

nws.noaa.gov/om/windchill

adventure.howstuffworks.com/survival/wilderness/how-to-avoid-hypothermia.htm

Planets and Moon:

photojournal.jpl.nasa.gov

crh.noaa.gov/fsd/?n=jupiter

Sun:

sdo.gsfc.nasa.gov/gallery/main.php

coolcosmos.ipac.caltech.edu/cosmic_kids/AskKids/sun.shtml

Vacuums and air pressure:

eo.ucar.edu/webweather/basic2.html

kids.earth.nasa.gov/archive/air_pressure

Rockets:

newton.dep.anl.gov/askasci/ast99/ast99044.htm

exploration.grc.nasa.gov/education/rocket/BottleRocket/Shari/propulsion_act.htm

Black holes:

nasa.gov/audience/forstudents/k-4/stories/what-is-a-black-hole-k4.html

Words of Thanks

Kudos to all of my family for their love and encouragement—I'm sure a fair number of them thought I'd never get this finished. "Extra" thanks to my wife Gera, my son Geraed and my sister Lisa for their support. My mom gets a big hug for being a faithful cheerleader with my projects over the years.   Dad, thanks for believing!

Special thanks as well to my storm chaser friends, those in the broadcast world, and anybody who offered kind words along the way. The well-wishes of others have been such a blessing during the countless hours I worked on this project. You're the best!

I'm also fortunate to have found Austin College graduate Elizabeth Cox as the artist for this book. She has an uncanny knack for interpreting my written words into some wonderful images. I think she'll go far and hope she remembers me when she's famous…

About the Author

Steve LaNore holds a Bachelor of Science degree in Meteorology from Texas A&M University. He is an AMS Certified Broadcast Meteorologist and is the Chief Meteorologist at KXII-TV, where he has worked since 2006. His television work also includes a 9-year stint in San Antonio and 6 years in Austin.

He has been awarded six times for broadcast excellence; "Weather Wits" received a 1st-place book award in 2012 by the Press Women of Texas for children's non-fiction.

LaNore lives in Pottsboro, Texas, a small community 60 miles north of Dallas, with his wife, Gera. His interests include weather, volcanoes, astronomy, history, music, travel, philosophy, and a good science fiction show. He is an enthusiastic blood donor and encourages all who can to give.

Steve LaNore links:

facebook.com/weatherwits

stevelanore.com

Contact Steve LaNore: science@stevelanore.com

About the Illustrator

Elizabeth Cox is a graduate of Austin College in Sherman, Texas.

She is a sculptress as well as an artist.

Contact Elizabeth Cox: e.obyrne.cox@gmail.com

59302523R00038

Made in the USA
San Bernardino, CA
03 December 2017